THE NATURE OF THE BEAST

Rochelle Foulk

The characters and events portrayed in this book are fictitious. Any similarity to real persons, living or dead, is coincidental and not intended by the author.

IBSN: 9798832560847

Cover design by: Art Painter
Library of Congress Control Number: 2018675309
Printed in the United States of America

This work is dedicated to God, my best friend, my lover and you.

CONTENTS

Author's Note:

The following is a real time account of what happened to me. I have spent two years writing this book, much of it spent in crying jags, drunken stupors, and random spiritual experiences. It's important the story is told accurately, because without accuracy there are no markers for the path. It is the path we seek, and sometimes we can lose sight of the path. That is when the miracle in the darkness happens.

I came to understand, through a power greater than myself, that I was on a journey paralleling Alice's adventures. The events happened in different orders. I would receive the answers before the questions. When I didn't know something I had this ability to reach into a data bank in my mind somewhere to come up with either "the answer" OR how to get to the "the" answer and the several answers before that point.

It was uncanny. Slightly unnerving at times and overall the most amazing and the worst 2 years of my life, to this point.

I sought help from all areas. Psych docs, my parents, med docs, strangers, God. With the rapidness of everything happening I realized writing was the only way to save my sanity. I am still maininting a wellness plan, got my team and my peeps. So, it makes more sense each day that passes how imperative it is I write this down. Some of it I will be seeing for the first time, alongside you. This will explain the changes in tense, vocabulary and voice.

Also, I need to introduce the writers. Some people call it multiple personalities, or another version of a mental illness. It is however just a willingness to see, hear, and follow. I call them guides, as it were they seem to be all doing that, guiding.

First, Rj, which I believe is actually a split of my personality. Rj developed during the last two years, the start of this book and several others. Rj and I don't always seperate when we speak. I believe the more accurate description of Rj is he is my male, I am his female. We are the twin spirit, Heyoka.

Quantum - feels like me, but I believe Q is a guide coming from the Andromeda Constellation (My People) and emissaries from the Pleadian Galaxy Network. They are all in an alliance with several other human type entities. I beleive 22 of them. Alex Collier has more information on this.

God - This is really God, what I mean is I communicate with God like Neale Donald Walsch described in his book; Conversations With God: An Uncommon Dialogue.

Jesus, The Christ makes His appearances too because He is my Savior.

I think that's everyone, however my name is Rochelle and I am them all and all are me. We exist for the purpose to light the way for others. I work for the Offices of the Christ. I am the Scribe, one of God's writers. I am here to guide those who need it, looking for it, and remembering who they really are.

My people, however are not all roses and candy. We are the ones they have forgotten, beaten, chewed up, spit out, killers, lovers, sinners, and the children.

I am Love's Champion. I am Hope. I am Love. I am a daughter of Christ and Mary. I am God's soldier. I am God's pen. I am God's instrument of Mercy.

This is my job, in the Universe. The PR man for Cosmic

Employment.

Remember, I warned you up front. This story will change lives. Take a leaf from our Boy Scouts, be prepared, always.

May God bless you and keep you in all ways.

So much color

I hope I'm not drunk. Was I at all?

You took my hand, my friend.

It's been many moments, since I've seen you.

And Him, since… Oh my goodness.

And here I am.

Repaint the karmic death.

Because I made a mistake?

Everything happens for a reason.

Maybe, there was a reason for this too.

You can say , I can say, I healed.

THE NATURE OF THE BEAST

In the natural world a beast is considered wild, untamed and free. An animal like a lion. These natural beasts and others are not hunting for trophies, or fame. They are killing for survival, for food, for territory. They are all doing exactly as they have encoded. The same is true with the other animal in this Kingdon. Man, all versions, the evolution of the Human.

The Beast however is what most refer to as an entity known as Satan, Lucifer, Beelzebub, and many more. The Beast is set to rule this world because it was given for contest so many eons ago. The only problem with that is there is no Beast outside of our current mythologies around the world. The only place the Beast does exist is here, points to head and or points to Heart. There will always be a beast in the hearts of Men for God saw it and made it known. The number of the Man is the same as the number of the Beast. Thus, Man is of the beast and grows from there.

Before you ask, my information comes from you, well the You, you. I consult God for clarification.I received some of my understandings of Christ and God through the Bible, Music, and Love. Mostly, my perception is from all the "nots". What ever 'they' did was what "not" to do.

I discovered, for myself, understanding the mechanics of something gives me an insight to the issue, problem, or people. I honed this skill during my youth and for thatpurpose, I am a Master. When one becomes a master then they must teach; for truth comes with knowledge. And your labor can not be reviewed until you see the eyes of your grandchildren. Then you will know if you raised yours, righteously.

So when I learned of the Beast it was not through normal or mainstream channels. I learned of it through the victims of MLK ultra and others apart of *that*. I found out that in order to control a population they need something to push them forward. If this what you do, then you understand. If its not what you do this insight will help you.

Because Fear is constant, accepting it makes *you* stronger. While the world's religions did their best to keep us moving forward. Little was done to counteract the Beast. I believe this comes from a limitied understanding of prophecy. Jesus's teachings and the greed of Man. He who controls the information, controls you.

How do we stop that?

It is what we need to do [society] especially if America is to fulfill her promise to the world.

First, acceptance. Know what is and what is not. Challenge yourself to look beyond the veil.

The quickest way to let go of everything you know,is imagine for a moment, everything you know is wrong. What ever your beliefs or whatever you think is just wrong. What do we do when nothing fits right?

Our ancestors thought forcing a round peg in a square hole was the answer. In retrospect, the holes are the wrong shape. So why continue pushing? Find another hole or another peg. Let go of what you know to embrace something new.

This will be hard. Some of you will not get it. Its okay, those not moving forward, remake the earth in their image. The rest move forward to the new earth. Its all very cosmic, really.

What is the lie they told you? Have you figured it out yet?

Does it feel, strange confusing? Do you find yourself staring off into space? Can you keep a house clean? Do you shower every day? How are your sleep patterns? What are you eating and how often?

These questions are what you focus on. They will lead you back to Yourself.

Somehow the programing is skewed or fried. You try, again and again. Relationship after relationship, job after job, apartment after apartment, animal after animal, and some plant after plant yet, nothing satisfies the void in your souls.

We have hit the bottom, there is one, obvious, truth.

There is no where else to go, save up.

That space in your heart that hurts, that bleeds, that reminds you this place will chew you up and spit you out for the dogs to eat.

That space right there. That is the **Lie**.

Whether someone told you this lie, or *you* tell you this lie; it is still the lie. Which means everything you know is actually wrong, or in this case not 'wrong' just backwards.

Yep, its inverted. So the Y-axis controls are in effect,people. If you understand my words, heed what they say, what they mean, Mother.

Up is down, Left is right, Down is Up, and Right is Left.

-Yeah, I know cross the eyes and roll your head back, go on then. The most important thing *I* can do is write about my experiences. Because without a record; its just bi-polar rants with a habitual ADHD streak.

Seriously, when reading and the sentences start to make no sense. Don't Panic, and grab your towel. When it confuses you just stop, take a breath and begin again, and see it with the filter "how to instructions."

The entity known as Satan is a created mythology by Catholics, christians, Judiasm, Muslim, and many others. They all have a version, which tends to lend credibility to the story.

What if the story was wrong, in that parts of it manipulated so that we walk ourselves into the trap?

The Beast is cunning, we created him. Then God sent us a weapon; Jesus Christ.

Its like playing a video game, modding it out so you can have God Mode. One shot, one kill.

IRL this equates to having the Christ as your shield, sword, armor and insight.

The Beast was created to keep you moving forward. Something to remind you of what lies behind. Its a backwards glance, people, not a forward one.

When Jesus met with Satan in the Garden of Gesamine, this is where they talk about Jesus communing with His Father. It is said, He met and talked with Satan there. Then defeated him with Death/Resurrection.

That is a tale of beasts, wizards, and a hero. Don't ya think?

My heart believes in Christ, no doubt. Do not get it Twisted.

My issue came when I attempted to go to these churches, read their books (bible) I found so many contradictions and false statements I left feeling dejected. I have the ability to hear God, we all do actually. It takes time to practice then it becomes as natural as breathing. Hearing the Word spoken is meant to uplift, nuture and release you from your sorrow, pain, and despair.

Sermon after Sermon I sat, taking notes, mumbling under my breath. One paster, the junior taking over for their Preacher. He was on a retreat with all the youth, in Indiana. I am not certain those children are treated well.

Any way, this young man spoke of Bosheba and the Harlot.
A story of a man who was told to go find a wife in this place, which was populated by prostitutes. Basically their version of a Red light District. The pastor went on to say, God commanded the man to go get the Harlot and marry her. So he did. Then she leaves and goes back to Harlotting. or whatever. Then man is commanded to go back and get her. Now, the pastor focused on the hardships of this man. He had to endure ridicule, scorn, and take from an unclean area. This Man was so horrified to have to do this. But he followed what god said to do.

The Pastor begged us, pleaded with us to see the plight of this man and how horrible it was for him. Then asked us to pay for the price that Jesus gave us. Basically pay for the blood that was spilt for you. Give it to us, the East Valley Baptist Church. So we can buy houses, and land to sequester more children on. Why?

-So that they have a fresh supply of breeding women?
Yeah, not buying that Salvation ticket.

So it seemed I did not find God in these Churches. I found god, the man who makes himself the Master, Lord, then Father. The whole time believing He is God and God leads him to shephard you.

I guess pedophilia is not screened for in Pastorial School.
It amazes me that no one else sees it. They were all sitting there, matching suits, Elders, Ushers, young children to the front. Women to the rear.

I still got Baptized there, I know, I know... my friends couldn't even walk in the building...
I still did, because God told me too.
Everyone laughed that night, because I slipped in the pool.
Turns out God has a sense of humor.
Or rather Love and Laughter outdo Fear and Sorrow any day of the week.

I am His vessel. and We made them laugh.

God bless those people and their pastor, please.

The next chapter is going to discuss what a parable is and the most famous one used to control Americans. I mean to say I am focused on America as my country is drowing. (I believe in her and you.) This is me helping to lift us up once more.

A Parable is a simple story that illustrates a moral or spiritual lesson. The difference between a Fable and a Parable is that fables use animals, personified. A parable uses angels or messengers from God.

That is it. So the story of Adam and Eve is a parable. Which means its a story of our creation, our existence in this world. Conciousness.

The details in the story have been changed to ensure patriarchial rule, this automatically disqualifies the original story because it doesn't include everyone.

That is the only rule. It must include everyone. All. The killers and Lovers alike.

Chapter Two: The Parable of Adam and Eve

Please note* No actual people were there or harmed in the making of this parable.

This particular story serves several purposes. First the terms Adam and Eve are names to remember the Sun and the Earth. Then to see Adam and Eve as beasts that evolved from natural evolution. This civilization didn't actually exist. The only part of human evolution that is difficult to track is sexual reproductive history.
Bloodlines, in otherwords. So while yes there was a male beast and a female beast, they weren't walking in some garden naming things and eating apples. It is the story of consciousness. Which if told properly, creates a much different picture of humanity. This is the story I am rewriting with the new perspective given to me by God.

Here is the current Christian version so that we start from the same place.

Eve ate an apple that the Serpent cunningly tricked her into. She takes the apple to Adam and beguiles him to eat the apple. He does. And then they were naked and afraid. Now ,God comes and calls out to them. They are freaking out and trying to dress in leaves not understanding why they are naked or how to make fig leaves fashionable. And here's what happened.

Adam and Eve come before God and are questioned concerning this new behavior of clothes. God asks if they ate of the fruit of the tree that he commandeth them not to eat of it? What is Adam's response? She made me do it. I am not making this up, Adam says

"The woman you made for me gave the apple and I did eat." So God turns to the Woman (Eve) and asks her why she ate of the fruit. Eve responds, "The serpent talked me into it." Then God turns to the serpent. God spoke to the Serpent , "Because you have done this you are cursed above all livestock, insects and animals of the earth. On your belly you shall go and dust you shall eat all of your days."

Now the rhetorhic here is interesting, God then tells Adam because you have listened to your wife and not your God you will work the rest of your days to make your food. The toil of the Earth, from it you came and return it you will.

God tells Eve she will experience pain in all her labor and childbirth. And she would have to serve Adam, her husband all her days. Then everyone is kicked out of the Garden and the way is shut by flaming swords, fire breathing dragons, and of course flying angels.

I am gonna sum this up right quick. When Daddy came home and asked who got into the apple pie, Little Adam points at his girlfriend? Seriously? and Then the girlfriend says the snake made me? And we get to hear the snake's version/punishment? And the blame falls at the feet of women because she gave you the apple. And the serving note there became our soul contract between men and women. We were taught to believe this and it *was* for lack of a better term, law.

Here's the thing, none of it ever happened. Listen, I am not downing Christianity, quite the opposite. There was this power to heal people, to bring people together and this Religion fought in the Name of Righteousness Sake.

And according to the beautitudes," Blessed are those who persecute for the sake of righteousness for theirs is the kingdom of heaven."

I know the written word was a knew thing and how to translate divine and holy expereinces with a small vocabulary can be frustrating. Its entirely possible something got screwed up in the translation. Because, well they couldn't be serious about this idea. So I dove back in, and found the same type of story "creation" in the Hebrew text and the Jewish text.

Hebrew is where the record is kept for the story of Moses/or Exodus. This is an **actual event** in *our* Human History.

They have found artifacts, even solved all 10 plagues God unleashed Eygpt, scientifically. The Hebrew texts, accounts and letters were retold for over 400 years before Jesus of Nazereth walked the Earth.

Jewish because they were ordained 'God's chosen people' and their charge was to study the scripture. For everyone else, as is stated in the Bible. . They are a nation of priests that are completely supported by their country and it's people to do this *one* job. And last but not least, Rome or rather Latin and Catholiscism. Why?

The Vatican is one the largest corporation in the world,with their own country and army. They have been in existence for over 1500 years. They being the Catholic Church which is who created the Vatican, the Vatican City, and other fun stuff.

Knowing nothing of God, save my own personal experiences, learning about the God through these major civilizations gave 'God' a whole new face. Allbeit the wrong one, but yeah, a whole new face.

Basically the people in charge of the spiritual growth of our planet also wrote the book how to get there,

*points up.

That book, however, is a compilation album. Its the best of the letters, sent to the apostles from each other. They discussed their specific areas and charges. They spoke of how to help them [the people]. They were cemented in that bond of brotherhood. These men walked the earth with Him. They heard Him speak and they spoke like Him.

These are the experiences of *their* understanding of God, *as* they understood Him.

That book, is Holy, and it contains the:

Basic

Instructions

Before

Leaving

Earth.

Our dear friend, Man [Read Adam} came upon some trouble they say, while walking in a garden one day. The one called Woman, mate of Man {read Adam} met a serpent. The serpent lived in the same garden. The Garden of Life Everlasting, granted through the grace of Spirit

It is home to all living creatures on the Earth.

The serpent is suppose to represent the begining of the Enity known, now, as Satan. Nothing exists *here* without Light &Dark.

(Gensis 1:Verses1-4) for the Almighty, Yahweh spoke life into the Universe for us to flourish, grow, and become.

Its meaning comes from understanding God as Love instead of Fear. God loves you, just as God loved the Earth and made it for us. So it stands to follow that once the choice of consciousness was made, we [Humans] began.

Thats it. The Garden is where you stand. You are the life planted here. The tree still exists because it is the tree of Knowledge. That tree explains all of the Universe, or gives you the awakening to search for said knowledge. God put the tree there, God also put the Serpent there, and finally God put Us there. What is the meaning of God giving you the Serpent in your own garden?

Beause it exists. To *not* show you would be to dishonor your potential. The **others** seek to uplift your fear so that it overrides your love for God, Earth and each other.

The greatest lie ever told is "it cannot be done". Its just the way that it is. *shrugs shoulders.

Nope. I don't uby that bullshit. Its sounds like a cop out on life. Like, well give up then, and toe your line. *raises eyebrow.

It is now UNDONE. In Jesus name, I manifest. Thank you God.

The turning of the mind against the Beast. Against that which we created for control. Against others that would seek to supplant God with Evil. We exist, here.

The rest of the world hasn't caught on yet, they don't know what's coming because they haven't prepared for the Event. As the Plandemic committe is referring to it. They are actually planning to bring Christ back and then ordain someone as King, probably.

Its corruption at the highest levels, who knows what the heaven they wanted. Those people, the Clintons, The Bushes, Bill Gates, and others have been killed.

That is what they are telling the xtreme right.

They aren't wrong but they ain't right either.

Its a circle game. Round and round we go, where it stops nobody knows. Trade your freedom? For what? For anything? Because that is what is happening. Take and then tell you what you need to hear to stay in *fear.*

Its a circle. The same game with new players. Same script different actors. This is not real. This is the illusion. And you are the only hope we have to ascend. We must Ascend. Going forward is the purpose of each life that is lived.

We move the world baby, *points to the crowd.

We do.

We are the chosen ones. We are responsible when anyone anywhere reaches out a hand for help. I pray, the Hand of God picks you up,in Christ's name; and for that; I am responsible.

Okay summing this all up, the eating of the apple is the representation of Us waking up, here. We were dressed, given tools, and eventually we became Neanderthals. There is no difference between us, and there are no lines of color, status or class. We are all Human, and through Christ we are Saved and we can turn this world into Heaven here as up there. *Points up

Chapter Three: Understanding evolution of the mind

Joseph Campbell, the world's foremost expert on Mythology wrote the Voyage of a Hero. It is a publication and the basis for Roddenberry's Star Wars Series. Myths, legends, fables, tales and stories are more than categories, they are units of measurement. What it measures is spiritual consciousness of the population in units of Time.

This spiritual consciousness is a source of power that when channeled properly can provide everything we need to survive. Energy, power, food source production, weather stability, the earth healed. Things of this nature. We, as the evolved species, [of] Human's no longer seek to Hunt, Subdue, or Defeat. The earth is ours, we have won and the prophecies of Old have come to pass. You stand in the Garden of Everlasting Life, right now.

We have seen the good and the bad of our pasts, our histories and our legacies. We wish to know more, to gain more, to give more so that others may rise at their chosen time intervals. We are the ones who raise the bar for the next generations.

For the Alpha Generation has been born. They are here, the future of our civilization as a species. And it is up to us, now, to raise the bar so that they [Alpha] may climb higher than we ever could on our own.

Success is often a category used to measure a person's wealth. This is true, however the 'wealth' subcategory is one of many within the Master School. One must enter said school and complete *all* module training programs in order to achieve its "Mastery" making You, unto others ,a teacher.

This process takes many, many lifetimes. For the value of something is determined by its deficits to the soul. If the value of something weighs the soul down then it becomes a deficit.

One must seek to rid of these weights so that they began to rise again. The process is arduous, tedious and not for the faint of Heart. For only true warriors brave these quests. Those of you who understand are now ready to shed the unnecessary weights and heal the Soul's wounds. This is done by a three-step process.

Acknowledge. Decide. Gratitude.

It is no less 'easy' than learning to tie your shoe the first time. A guiding hand helps to prepare you for this task, until the task is complete one cannot move forward, as it were.

This is why I am here, to help provide the way through this rising of Christ, which is going to lead to a massive shift in consciousness for the Planet. As with all things one must journey forward first in order to become the guide for others to follow. The first is the Beacon, seeing the beacon is more difficult than one realizes. The Beacon changes and warns you of dangerous shore lines. The Beacon is a way point marker on your soul's journey. The Next is a space existing simultaneously with your reality. The curtain, or veil, becomes transparent. You will see into the lives and the hearts of others. You will get a sense of knowing that was not there previously. This is part of the evolutionary change and the next step for our species, humans.

It is a concept you have been practicing for several decades now. How and when to take responsibility for others. This is no small ask, and to become a person who leads others towards safety in the event of a crash landing you will have to complete a master school. That 'Job' as we like to call them requires cunning of the mind and a warrior's spirit, two things that are harder to come by than you realize. When the merging begins we must atone for all that was done to us and from us. It is of utmost importance to understand what 'merging' is prior to beginning its inception. Taking responsibility is a skill to increase, another subcategory. All good gamers know, skills take time, effort and willingness to increase. That's why we fight the enemy over and over again. It build's experience. This is the arcade version,my friends, one quarter, three lives.

All of it spins together and creates "your path" unto the Universe. Each of the mythologies Campbell visited had a connection to each other he discovered. One of the greatest discoveries for Humankind. Joseph Campbell found that each one had a creation myth, a flood myth and the next highest ranking was the Virgin Birth. Campell after years of study created a new mythology, ours. The next evolutionary spiral is coming and unification is our only hope for survival. What comes will be remembered as the wrath of God. That is absolutely correct, however we also know it as turning the spaceship. Now, what makes the planet move?

Magnets.

Very big, large fields of magnetic energy to be more precise. These fields are what create the physical universe we experience every day. Every proton, neutron, and electron carry a signature frequency. Sound is the Holy Spirit incarnate thus music unleashes within you, through you and all around you. Or for our extra credit winners, taking speed to do it faster. I don't know about you but sober is hard enough, mK? The planet moves within these fields of energy and it is a slow, I mean like the sloth at the DMV in that movie, Zootopia? That slow. That is what makes these a very important junction in our evolutionary history. Because the Omega Generation has been born too. Do you know when Alpha and Omega appear what happens, right?

The Big Bang Theory.

Sigh, yeah, I mean I was a little shocked at first but then I remembered Futurama. They watched the world end and then began again. Just like that. That got me thinking, like really thinking about this whole creation mythology in the first place. Sometimes looking at things in a bigger perspective enlightens the areas unseen from the ground view. This implies, perception is everything when you are looking through a microscope. That is the most accurate description I can come up with on how to access your deity strength. I am hoping to get it into the games.

Basically, every mythology on the planet aligns with the religions and theologies of our current day. Again, the word religion is a subcategory with its own subcategories. Each has a master school assigned and all do not have to be completed to move through to the next level. Each Soul must master three. You may always do more, however you can not do less. At least not on this plane. We have entered into the next realm of existence. This is called Dimension 5, or if you prefer the 5th Dimension. The shape correlated to the Fifth Dimension is a Diamond. Specifically, the geometric design of the Diamond as it is depicted in symbols. For most of us, an upside-down triangle will do, meaning its enough to see it as the pattern associated with the shape "Diamond". This dimension as well as others have rules, each rule is set to be a marker. Markers are path way markers, a beacon if you will. Stepping outside the Marker is always a choice, you get every choice, every time. The Marker does not move. They stay the line so that those who approach can find their way.

The Marker can speak to you, and will when it becomes necessary. There will be times when the Marker will talk to you and what it says doesn't jive with your vibe. Its up to you to choose whether to accept the offer or to decline. The choice is always yours. Along the way of these Markers, you will find the next intersecting path. Many of us have difficultly here, physically speaking it's the pit in your stomach, anxiety. That is a precursor to a panic attack as it happens; *recognition* is your torch. Seeing the enemy as an outline of the truth. When we see something, it automatically changes its direction. This is the basis of Quantum Mechanics. It is called the Observer. When the Observer sees the Marker, theye can speak unto his brother. These junctures create steps to ascend the ladder of evolution. All steps are created, that means we create them as we go. God only made the Heavens, the Earth and the Universe. Everything else? That's up for grabs. If you look for what father made you then you can see the Word in everything, and I do mean everything.

We are at this juncture, now. Creating a new step in the evolution of our species, Human. This a category also, known to you as Species Category. We see that as a sub category now. Under the Species: Human there are two kinds of Humans. Only two. It is these two that will always move forward. They are already spoken for and belong to Christ. No other has any power over Him.

There are requirements in order to create the step. For example, permits, licensing's Mastery Schools Assessment (MCA Number.), mine is a six. During this process several things happen to the individual applying for the permits. The CEO, as it were, to orchestrate such a large rebuilding process. The Contract itself is enormous. Never mind the cost in materials. It is, however, what must be done if we are to survive. And by that, I mean still exist.

The first mythology is the creation of humans. The Christians would have you believe a Man was created with the breath of life and the sands or dirt of the Earth. Jewish Faiths hold the entity in the creation fable was Hermaphroditic. Then there is the Hebrew version, which depicts the creation of man/woman as a creature that has male on one side and female on the other side. AS if they were connected back-to-back. That sounds really close to that horrible horror flick Centipede.

The two that always move forward are male and female.

Thats it. Now, here is where people get freaky. Pay close attention now, its phrasing is simplistic and genius.

Two - Male/Female

Male energy/Female Energy

Synergistic, yin and yang.

in one body.

So, if I am not mistaken, every person falls into these c ategories, regardless of transgender. Stay with me, now, remember we are looking through the lens "what we know is wrong or inverted". Which means we have to revert back to God. Or if you wish, the Universe.

We aren't talking bits and parts here, people. We are talking about Energy, Consciousness, and Ascension.

Chapter Four: The birds and the bees...

The Creation of humans is an ongoing evolutionary process, we all began from the one, true Dyad; Male/Female.

This is the primary dyad for creation. The Universe is built in threes, leaving us to fill in the equations.

We start with the first one, Male/Female.

All life springs from this pairing. This pairing exists since the beginning creation, even with the planets and the trees everything. For the dyad to exist it must have markers to guide the path for it's progeny.

For right now, we are focusing on Human life, its creation and its continued evolutionary progress..

If F/M = Life, then F+M= C (child)

Which is another way of saying 1+1= 3.

Think about it; one man, one woman, then baby, that's three people.

As an ordered pair, (F,M) the balance of inner engery can be measured. Using a grid and positive/negative movements that take us from (0,0).

Simply because we have named them M and F, and they are two seperate entities; we also create the other two sets of variables that form the markers

They are M/M and F/F, or male/male and female/female. All three exist simultaneously, all three contribute to the evolutionary process of the Human.

The three points, drawing a triangle. It looks like an upside V. The point of origin is where you start.

That is the M/F variable, which the start of life. Then the Origin connects to each of it's Markers, in this case F/F and M/M this creates the trifecta of all human life.

We are all responsible for every human on the planet. Mark my words, every Human, on the *planet.* A person's point of Origin as we have already discussed, in my previous book; is You to Earth to God.

Not Jesus. He is *not* God.

He is *only* Lord when He comes back.

That was one version. One of Many. In fact, all over the Globe there is a version of this same-type story. The Prophet who came to predict the father. The Prophets that led slaves from Egypt.

It is the same story. The same 'voyage of a hero' that Campbell created based on all the mythologies of the world.

The next question, or deterrent if you will is that your mind is actually telling you it's *not* the same.

Right now, as you read the words, I type your still doubting this.

I call this the "response".

The "response" is a triggered reaction that produces the programing you were given. Be it Catholic, Satan, Pagan, Christian, etc...

This "response' was engineered through a psych operation that people endured after WWII. It has been named as MLK Ultra . This came from the experiments Hitler did in WWII. Every country that was an Ally, took and parted out all of Hitler's discoveries, results, and experiments.

We, U.S.A, used them on our own people. Here in the continental United States. This is what happened, I am simply repeating what has already been revealed.

If you are asking yourself why, what would be the possible reason to do that to our own people.

Easy- Control the population, control buying and spending power of a Nation. Pay for the money they borrow to buy the products we made then make them pay us more through Credit. That is Power, my friends. If someone has the power to let in companies or providing things Americans consume then there is someone who signs off.

If there is a person in charge, that person is corruptible. The military solved that problem by using two person integrity. The forefathers remedied that by instituting a 3 branch system of government. We have been fighting for a long time to be free of this Global market and maintain the Free Trade Market.

What's it come back to? Money, Power, Control, all for the purpose of winning?, I guess.. Personally its too much headache to want to control everyone. Shit its hard to just control the people in my life. Which ironically, I just learned is NOT how to love them.

Let them go. Let them breathe. Let them live. Let them thrive.

We have terms to delineate time for example, Antique means 100yrs or more. Vintage means at least 20 years.

Myths, legends, and fables are all measurements of Time.

That is their specific purpose, to provide the record of human evolution. Which is exactly what the Bible is;

An anthology of human evolution.

Jesus on the Cross?-That symbolizes the Last Sacrifice.

None need be slaughtered in the name of God, for God gave us their only Begotten son; Jesus of Nazareth born to Joseph and Mary.

Jesus is Savior for Mankind. - reads all human life/animals/Earth.

His last sacrifice freed us All, from ALL slavery.

It **is the first** Emancipation Proclamation.

Quantum/God-Which doesn't actually mean that everyone stopped sacrifices. There was a cool off period after the death and resurrection of the Christ. That was saracastically written. Actually, we call it Hungry Hippo's; like the child's game. From lightyears away under a microscope, discernable shapes are impossible. Thus we named them in accordance to their collective behavior. The Christ, Ascended to the Creator and BAM! Dark arms flung out spreading all the way around the surface of the planet. We, of course are watching it speed lapsed, so its like every second would be 10,000 years. So if you wanted to go faster, you would increase the amount of time in between each reveal. There is another level to this vision, where we watch the time lapse through multiple perceptions, with an exponential speed.

Rochelle (Rj)-Of course, they didn't, I mean from a sales point of view someone has now given the Opposite of your original Product. So, the pitch goes, "It is a sin to lust. It goes against God but if you repent in the Lord you shall be forgiven."

Quantum/God -That was off the top of your head?

Rj/ - Yeah, but let's break it down, shall we?

Quantum/God- Please, I am excited to see you translate this one.

Rj/ You know your an ass, right?

Q/God Ah yes, I do love your pet names for me.

Rj - *Shakes head and begans again.

The subject: Sin has been identified as Lust. Lust is defined by the feeling you get when you look at a woman. (They were talking primarily to Men.) So, the feeling is also known as Puberty, Hormonal Rages, and well Lust. This "sin" can be forgiven (nullified) through admitting to the act/thought/feeling. This progressive thought process created the following pattern:

--*She looks so good, I have to have her.* Thought

Takes girl and pins her down, plunges himself into her and out of as if it will satisfy this rage.* Fantasy, thus word and thought combined to create.

"A local teacher has been found near her residence, dead."

The thought, the fantasy became a reality but only one person created the reality.

We call that: The Beast.

It is *your* primal self, the parts of you that helped to create the world's population. The stronger you feel these feelings the stronger your soul. A strong soul can apply for jobs in the Universe. Its called Cosmic employment.

Quantum/God - You have been paying attention. You are correct, though the job description doesn' t use the terms 'rapists, colonizers, etc'. Those are Human terms to describe human behavior based only on your knowledge and observation. We are seeing the behavior of Conquest in congruence with primitive religions, cultures and tribes.

When we quantify our data it is similliar to your scentific method and statistical analysis. We see the same behavior, over and over.

For example, this particular behavior : Conquest, it is consistently how you[Terrans} have recreated yourseves for nearly billions of years. Attack, take, use, give away, bring back, hold on, eat, and reproduction style are all examples of Conquest.

When *this* thought process is triggered, then repeated in others, by the rules of creation you multiplied by multiple minds. This is how these behaviors are coded into your DNA.

Rj- Wow, that was intense, I was here when you wrote that but also not. What happened?

Quantum/God - You have opened with full intention and accepted your role here on earth, Rochelle. For that we are grateful.

Rj- I am honored. *Quantum raises a glass

The Beast, often slapped on the wrist and set free because he is the Beast. All men respect the Beast because they too, know the Beast. The Beast is you, always has been. We evolved from this Planet. Which we all know means bacteria, amoebas and mitosis. NO actual people walked around in a Garden. *That* is the vision of Heaven, **Given**. This vision may not line up with your personal views but it never had too.

Life is a Garden, baby. Dig it.

The Beast evolves from survival instincts, which based on circumstances can mean anything. So far, We, man and woman, have evolved into the versions of God so depicted in this mythology of Adam and Eve. Evolution, however, is not only on one plane. Where the physical form has become its perfected piece of today. The Spiritual form is also necessary to evolve.

If it doesn't you get what we had here, last year.

Bingo Cards for 20/20

Pandemic

Plandemic

Death

Division

Break Point

Rebuild

That, my friends, is the acutal plan, being spoke of though many channels, networks, non-mainstream, outside networks. It causes the: confusion, panic, multiple fronts fighting each other and not one voice of hope.

Its the same program that is used in raising the children of the Baby Boomers, later named Generation X. Your wecome.

We stopped the breeder's plans. We pushed for mental health awareness. We marched for civil rights, womens rights, special populations, and LGBT rights. We stopped the traditions that killed our spirits. We pretended, to make it better for others. We stood the line against the monstors we knew. In everyone we knew. We hold the line for American Freedom. We learned it from our Parents. They had been fighting for nearly 30 years at this point. They fought for civil rights. They fought for feminism. They fought against the establishment. They even fought for LGBT.

They mostly, however, had to focus on the laws, structures that would help their children climb a little higher than they did. They fought for their parents, who raised them just as hard as they raised us. Why?

Because in the efforts to steer a country to her glorious destiny, some found the lure of money, power, sex, and greed overwhelming. They chose to walk across the line and pick them. At that moment, ladies and gentlemen, is when one commits Treason.

This is no small act. Treason is the very thing that will bring us to our knees. The reason for that lies in our evolution as a country.

I have good news. The ones responsible for continuing the slave trade of American Citizens have been dealt with.

Read that anyway you want.

Treason, however has been committed. At the highest level. It has been written into our laws. It has been sown into your DNA coding. And last but not least, you have been fighting to keep it.

That leads us to the Ugly Playground. Remember the motto, Always be Prepared. Sempre Fi.

Evolutionary History

Okay, I am writing at the time point of when I entered into the 7th dimension. The date is May 6th, 2022. I have begun the building process. My work will be completed by the time of my death. Even though most will not understand for a long time. From this space I can reach into the 5th dimension to pull the Line forward. It is my destiny, my fate, my Love, my privilege, my job, my commitment to you. For we all exist simultaneously, we always have, The Next will give you Sight. And what you will See, you cannot Unsee. Some of you will be lost in the translation, fear not for the Lord has prepared a place for you. In God's name Jesus will come to save his People, always and in all ways.

For the rest, you will have begun your Karmic Journey into the Next. This is a normal transition for Sentient Beings. For this is the train station you choose your purpose, destiny or fate. Everyone does get here. Everyone gets here on their Time. Forgive yourself in favor of forgiving all.

We are the evolution of Humanity, however when a civilization reaches this point they must decide where they will go. This is Law and incontestable among the Mortals. Entrance into each Dimension/Garden you will submit to the Divine Law. Plain and simple. The reason: this is the way it is - [created by God.] And it makes sense if you understand how the Mechanism works.

You do know how the Mechanism works. It works the same way Life does, except you don't know the words to speak. It has been kept from you, the path to your Ascension. This happens by design and helps to transition the soul through the 4,5, and 6 dimensions. The point you are at now will require your Ascension from 3rd to 4th. I can no longer see 3rd dimensionals because the Fractal has turned twice. They however can see me, if they are looking, only from their view I am either Good or Evil. You can only see to the choice you haven't made. The Same is for all plus or minus 2.

The Next is the place you have called Heaven, Eden, Higher Consciousness. These are not the correct terms simply because they do not come close to what Heaven actually is. Partly because the words do not exist yet.

Fear not for the Lord walks with you, He shall preserve you. The Ascension into the next dimension is the choice to be made here. For some the choice is easy and they rise without contestation. This is called Rapture. That can only happen if you have Ascended through the 3 schools of Mastery to get to Rapture. That is not easy. It is doable but it is not easy. This is why we call it Rapture. To the mortal eye it will look like something breaks into light and travels away. It will be as if by Magic, some will say. Others will call it divine. It makes no difference what you call it, for it is Known and thus cannot be discovered.

How you travel through the train station is also a choice. As you will soon understand, choice is everything. Even the illusion of Choice is good enough to satisfy the drive for humans. If you knew you had every choice available to you what would you say?

Quantum/God - And this is exactly why Awakening happens in stages. A rapid ascent/descent will cause physical damage to the current corporeal being. Souls are eternal, your body is not. This idea called Choice was created to give you the ability to experience anything you desired. Yes, I do mean anything. Bad and Good are constructs by Man (read Humans), in an effort to push our species forward we create rules for what we allow and what we don't.

In other words, the creator is Human Kind individuals, what you the creator make you the creator can destroy. It is in THIS way you are the likeness of GOD. And as you have seen, the image of GOD comes in many colors, styles, sexes, genders and sizes. Even intention is spoken for among us. Some will claim their rightful heritage and remain a Trafficker. Why? Because we haven't eradicated the black market. Will we do so? Probably not, most of us still believe that if you choose your life, it's your life.

The caveat here, I believe, is said best in American,

"You do you Boo. But, when what or who you do crosses my Line then you will have the wrath of a Creator upon you. "

The law was written, as it stands, that law [Lev. 19-21]; "an Eye for an Eye and a tooth for a tooth."

That law has not changed in over 2500 years. What I mean by change is that this law never changed a body part, or decided it was no longer necessary to exact payment for transgressions. This is still the Law, it is however Universal Law. An Eye for an Eye and a Tooth for a Tooth. Has it ever crossed your mind why? Why an Eye? Why a Tooth? What the heck was some dude trying to say when he chose to interpret God's word. Or Jesus's testimony? Before written language had rules, mind you.

The Bible, ironically, contains most of the answers I found. It must be noted, however, the Bible only contains partial truths. Each religion that has formed in the last 2000 years is vying for the spot of "The Word". They are finally realizing there is no such thing. And sadly through much bloodshed both morally and spiritually we are finally realizing the same truth. There is no difference between us, save the ones we created ourselves. Those falsehoods do not define the Human spirit. You do. Each of us, each one that survives, each one that stands up, each one that fights back. Each one of you defines Us, we do this collectively. It is our collective consciousness that creates entities like Satan, the devil, and other words to inspire the Fear.

This is part of the Mechanism too. Although it is the part they have not told us about, partly because they sought to hold the line for Humanity. They also succumbed to their own desires. And ultimately figure out what we know already, Absolute power corrupts absolutely. No one is better than another. God is the Alpha and the Omega. Therefore no one exists outside of God. As God is both the beginning and the end.

God is not a religion, definitions are important here, true meaning is necessary to manifest accurately. Once the concept of God becomes manifest in a civilization then it moves faster in its evolution. Basically as you would expect, if you get the right tools for the Job then the work is easy, swift and perfect. If you have no tools or knowledge of tools then the Job becomes a hardship, and eventually will kill you. This you already know, because this is also how Life works.

What is the Bible, really? Is it a book, yes it is a book. More accurately it is a collection of Letters, known as Epistles. These letters were sent to each of the Disciples of Chris from themselves. They told each other of the work they were doing all over the known world. These letters became books that later formed the books of the Bible. When you hear the word 'book' we all get this mental image in our minds. We also get an approximate length, thickness or even intelligence level of said 'book'. It is how your memory works with word association. Expansion of the Consciousness allows you to See what something is as it is instead of what you imagine.

For example, if I said, Dr Sues's latest release from the family's vaults produced a five book series on feelings, growing up, and such.

You may see a collection of Dr Suses colorful books, like One Fish Two Fish, Red Fish Blue Fish.

Or you may see a kindle with the electronic version. It's a technique we use to memorize, recall information, as well as create. It is also programmable by you or anyone else. They figured out how to do that through WWII.

They called it MLK ultra. And it was a perfectly executed plan because it worked. I know that because we are still here. Right now. We shouldn't be. Not based on the life I have lived in this Country. Not my individual life, no. I mean as a country, as states, as members of the international ring. There are so many ways this Country could have, may have and they are still trying too; fall.

It didn't. We are still here.

Why?

This was my quest, to answer the questions no one seemed to be able to answer let alone hear. My need to understand the problem in order to fix it comes from my personal life experience. Those 17 years of experiences trained me to do what I do today. Just as yours have trained you, or if you prefer, programmed you. The catch here is, and this is where it gets sticky, your programming, Training, is exactly how you get out of the playground. There are three things that rule over Evil. Only three, they are immutable and cannot be changed because they are given by the Creator. No matter what ANYone says, does, proves or shows you these three tools are your beginning arsenal.

You have woken up in the world, similar to the movies you have seen and it appears to be out of sorts. All around you people are acting differently. Some of our comedians and news anchors have already commented on this. It appears there are different realities simultaneously existing. Only now the veil between the dimensions is lifted. You now get to See all that has been manifested to this point. Here is where you choose what stays and what goes into the Next.

What are the three tools you begin with?

The first one is Gratitude.

The second is Jesus.

And the third is You.

Evil exists, and ironically the story is in the parable of Adam and Eve which if you read, comprehend, and meditate with God on the story's meaning.

That's it, our charge now is to teach you how we evolved into existence. We, meaning, Humans. We are not all humans out the gate. That is not how the story goes, which is the story of Genesis. Or the beginning of all Life in this Universe.

The Bible is an Evolutionary History, of our [Human] spiritual, emotional and metaphysical selves. From the beginning, The Alpha, there is a man, woman, serpent. This is a story mind you, not actual people or an actual snake. These are terms which can be used as a category as well as a singular function. Meaning Man/Woman are what we call Humans. There must always be the two, for without each other no life is created. That male/female pairing is not limited to one style of corporal being. The Soul can be either or both at the same time. This is true in our ecosystems, nature and our past earth. [dinosaurs and such]. The dyad is male and female, which is made in the image and likeness of God. They appear in all the forms you see now.

No ONE is God, we are all sparks of light, soul children of the One. Which we can call God, Creator, Great Spirit, Allah, Yahweh etc. There is no difference between them save the terms you have used. In the story a species of us, before we became the Human of today, lived and grew, procreated and ruled this planet. Those species of Humans grew from the earth. Scientifically this is explained through evolution of animals. Now the widely accepted versions concerning certain Apes is one of these. It isn't inaccurate, per se, it's just a vague overview slapped together for a first year college student. The reality of our DNA, genetics is still being discovered. However I can tell you that in the future they will teach that Humans were grown on the planet through the planet and of the planet. We didn't find this world. We are born of it, thus it is ours, granted by the Great Spirit to keep, dress, and grow.

We are all Earthlings, Terrans, Humans, Man, Sons and Daughters of Eve and Adam. Then reborn in Christ and Mary.

You are the keepers of the Garden.

We are the keepers of of the Way to the Garden.

We are all responsible for ourselves.

When we are responsible for self, then we can be responsible for others.

Eventually, they become responsible, and that is how a civilization is Born.

An Ugly Playground

When we, my brother, sister and our cousins played in the yard as children, there were lines we couldn't cross. Each line represented an age bracket. For example, for about three years we were not allowed out of the back yard. The Orchard was off limits, the side Pasture only to go home, and the Paddock were a few. As kids we were told we stayed there and couldn't go there *points to all the places, without an Adult.

This particular teaching is similar to raising horses and bulls. Also Dogs and other working animals. Children are like small animals in that they need a place to explore and learn.

The backyard became my playground. We [siblings including cousins] learned all the rules of that playground. We were stung by bees, dug in the pit where we butchered chickens, and roller skating for hours up and down a sidewalk that was only two and half feet wide and thirty feet long. I had two by two roller skates. They had red wheels and white leather. They were old but the bearings were brand new. I rolled up and down that sidewalk a thousand times if I did it once. Then there were the three wheelers, I rode that thing until I was 15 years old. This playground provided entertainment, learning curves and our little safe place to be.

When our parents, grandparents and great grandma sent us to play they knew beyond doubt where we would be because they trained us in all the playgrounds. By the time we were 8 my brother was building rope ladders to swing through the barn over the hay which was stacked forty feet high. I built walkie talkies by nailing roofing nails into a small piece of a two by four. I invented a game we played with all our cousins, I called it Spy vs Spy. Then there was Death before Dishonor. And finally when I was way older, I played a new game with my younger cousins. They still remember it to this day, The Gatekeeper.

My sister is my junior by about 6 years, she played and grew up with my younger cousins. This was one of the games we got to play before the way of Life separates you from your siblings. The games we played, the rules we learned, the hardships we endured, we did as a family.

It sounds great when I say it that way, and its supposed to. I chose to see it this way when I began forgiving my trespassers as God forgave me mine.

And *that* is how most of Gen X was raised. I worked, cooked, and cleaned by the age of ten. I could cook a three course meal for five by 12. And I knew how to change a tire and my own oil by 16. My brother learned more because it interested him, he later became a mechanic, stereo and speaker installer. He can make some great boxes. Even though there was segregation, physically intense punishments, psychological torture and the random sexual abuse. We still survived it as a family. We grew from it as a family. Did all the roses come out in the end? No. Was it supposed to? Also, No.

It happened. It also happened so often that talking about it only made us feel worse because then we knew the truth. As children you talk to other children, make no mistake this still happens today. The playground at school is where we learn social order, behavior and sports. We still talk to each other, some of us share our darkest secrets. Do you know what we found out?

It happened everywhere. Everyone went through similar things as we did, growing up. The more people I talked to the more aware this thought became. There was no escaping the pain, the torture, and the hunting. Even the cops did nothing. White or not, this is one line no cop crosses. Which is sad because that is exactly what the Cop is supposed to do. Humans rarely learn on the first go around.

When a generation realized that Sexual, Psychological, and Pyshical torture were not only allowed but rated by the lawmakers, sherrifs, judges, mayors, and Heaven Forbid the government. We knew then, just what our parents had been talking about.

The playground got ugly, only I think it's always been ugly because none of the women in my family have good memories to share. They speak as if they didn't exist and only the people of the time existed. It's a weird analogy but there ya go. Where are the memories? Where did you learn to rollerskate? Such questions brought haunted looks and far away voices lulling me with some story that didn't pertain to the question.

I can admit to you, during my journey of recovery from my childhood trauma I carried Hate, Revenge, Seething Wrath, and the ability to turn cold as Ice. My tongue was sharper than any pen, and my brute strength intimidated most. I used all the tools I learned growing up so I could survive out here. In the real world with you. Imagine my surprise when all of you were still sleeping. When only parts had awoken. Some things stopped making sense. Others became so crystal clear, I no longer needed anyones opinion or validation. I grew up, carried a bag of tricks with me and started being a member of Society. My anger towards my family, members specifically and the general population of America became all that I was. It consumed me and turned me into a version of my grandfather, my father, my grandmother and my Auntie.

I tried to take their good characteristics and build me a new personality that could live ...here. *points to the world. I thought if I remade myself, using all that I knew then I could have this 'life' everyone talked about. It was good, long, and fulfilling they said. They didn't sugar coat the truth of it either but turned a blind eye to the Evil growing under our feet.

When I hit my wall after Misha's death, I knew then I had been wrong. I knew where my heart was and why I couldn't reach it. So I gave up. Surrendered to the only thing I knew, vaguely but still knew.

From that day forth I am whole, human and here to serve in the best capacity I can for the longevity of the human race.

Turns out only God can make you. Everything else is just an imitation of the Original.

The Holy Spirit

She came to me. She loved me. And She showed me the way through this...Ugly Playground. I have played here, built forts, lived and died here. This is my playground, and I have brought my divine tools to share with my friends. She is His and they are the twin stars meant to light our paths unto Heaven here on earth.

The Playground is a metaphor for Life. It can be an ugly place. It is up to us to clean up the mess and allow others the same joy we experienced.

For this analogy, and its purpose which is to raise awareness levels by one. The Playground will help us translate knowledge into conception and experiential knowing. It will be important later in the production line of reality. The playground I refer to is not a personal one, in this playground we all exist. I am, now, accepting my role in this playground, my purpose and my Life as it has already been given.

The Playground is aptly named because we "play" with each other in it. The types of play that go on in a playground are all constructions of socially accepted behavior patterns for humans, males, beasts, females, trans-humans, demons, spirits, Angels, heroes, devils, and everyone else not sitting on a cushion. Here, we enact in these scripts, energy patterns, karmic debt repayment, and different roles so that we can decide what we will serve Us [Humanity] and what will not. We also learn how to move through those scripts in order to ascend to the next dimension of existence. The roles discussed in the Ugly playground are the “black spots”, “skeletons in the closet”, “the white elephant in the room”, or what we call the Unseen.

If you are to traverse this path, it is for a purpose unknown to you, personally. For these paths are only tread by those who have the training. Diving into a known, created Hell is similar to deciding that you now defend your country from the enemy. Except the “country” is actually Humanity and the “enemy” is actually Evil that takes the form of Humans in order to enact their purpose. Which if it is not known, the purpose of Evil is to Unmake God and All of God’s Children.

Rest assured, that is impossible, untenable and well quite rude if you ask me. Unmake existence? What kind of asinine plan does that make? Seriously, though, the way Evil gets in is through the choices we make with each other and these entities mentioned above. Are you ready? Do you have the tools to traverse recess? These and other questions will prompt your fear button, please regulate emotions accordingly.

Adjusting to the playground is a specialty of mine, some call it ``Chameleon like ' or "Ninja” due to how we change our appearance in such a way that we look “made to be there.” Many of us already know how to do this, or if properly described will understand it without having to relive any experience.

I chose Love early on, and focused all my thoughts on finding and being with Love. And now, through Christ Consciousness I have the background and the foreground of *my* existence. Combining everything together with God's wooden spoon, I began to mix.

Remember our original set of tools we are born with are Gratitude, Jesus, and You. You are divine and perfect in the image and likeness of God. Gratitude is a taught behavior that will unlock the Spiritual Realm. There is where you find your weapons, armor, tutelage, basically think "Magic portal to the place where Perseus got his Shield, Helmet and Sword. Or if you prefer,The Room of Requirement or any other video game analogy, sci-fi reference or a specific book."

It makes no matter what you call this place, its function is still the same: Restore, Replenish and Release. Some call it Nirvana, Shamballa, Heaven, Garden, Eden, and whichever ones I have left out.

It can only be gotten by giving thanks for what you have been given. All that you have been given.

Even that which you disdain, disown, discount, rebel from, shirk away, judge and of course kill.

All of it. For none of it matters if black lives don't matter.

Do you see the point?

Of course black lives matter, so do all the colors matey.

By the way, your inner child just said, "Duh."

All that is good and bad is Good. All things work for Good. Which if you like the "biblical route," Genesis Chapter 1, verse 4 and

Romans Chapter 8 verse 28; God said it was Good, the light and the dark. All things work for good.

Evil is not bad. Evil is Evil or life [LIVE] lived backwards. Which is another way of saying, "Undone, Unmake, or turn inside out." The reality is Evil believes, as in lives, for the ability to, unmake creation in order to suck the power from God. Evil believes it can do this. That is the battle we fight. That is the War which is almost over. This is what has been prophesied by all the major religions, Catholic, Christian, etc. It was also spoken in the ways of Pagan, the Occult, Druids and Pentacostal. It was before and it is now, the Word handed down to us by our ancestors, predecessors, and bloodlines. This is the fight for our very, precious right: Existence.

The Beast stalks in the night, the day, from the air and from under the ground. None know him but all fear him for he was spoken for in the time of Old. He is no more Evil than your grandmother but is more cunning that you know. For the Beast lives within you, it is your evolution of being. The man becomes the son and eventually the father. The woman becomes the mother and eventually the holy spirit. We are that from which we are made. From dust to dust, ashes to ashes, we all fell down.

There is hope, still waiting to be called. She lives in the box we buried long ago. For she stayed when the spirits joined the world. She alone believed in us and so she stayed and now we have hope. That hope, the last hope, is simply your belief that you are not your Father, You are not your Mother. You are the manifest of them through the love of God. No matter how your conception went, it was forced, pressed, pushed upon, demanded, given, it is still in God's Love you are made. So it was, as it has been and is from now till forever more. Amen.

You Honor thy Mother and thy Father by becoming better than each of them. Better serving, better met, better loved, you are more than they are because you come from both of them.

Honor does not mean obey. It never has, the meanings of the words we use are not subject to the rules of societal pressures. Grammar is still grammer. The accuracy in which the words are spoken lends to their weight in truth, gold, dust, and water. The definition of the word honor is high respect, great esteem. It also means an adherence to what is right or to a conventional standard of conduct.

Honor is a noun and a verb. Defining honor as a verb; regarding with great respect [recognizing another's part in your victory] and to fulfill an obligation or contract [ensuring one performs on their behalf like quality control].

Do you have to do this?

-No

Then why do it at all?

-because it is how to rise above the 'ick' associated with current programming tracks. -Quantum/God

Rj/Rochelle - Then why doesn't God make it mandatory? If I don't have to do it, then I won't. I wouldn't be caught dead anywhere near the people that hurt me. That is just too much to ask.

-This goes back to the first Universal Law. Free Will is Absolute. And it is Yours. A gift from the Creator. You decide which you want or don't want. You pick the ideas, concepts, reasons for things to happen in your life as well as the lives of others. God makes no mind over your choices, because you have the gift. Why would someone give you something and then watch you use it to determine if you are doing it "right"?

God wouldn't, because God is not Human, neither Man or Woman. The illusion of the son and the father and the Master? Those are not jobs of humans, men or women. Those are the jobs of Christ, the disciples and the saints. ITs called Free Will for a reason, your will cannot be broken if it is aligned with your Divine Will. Which is another way of saying, God's Will for you. Although that is an inaccurate statement. God's will is your will, because of the first Universal Law. All sentient beings know this as you know the word freedom. It has become an experience we willingly invite in because it serves us. Thus God's will is your will, your Divine Will is that of your Higher Self, Higher Consciousness, Supreme Being, God's Direction, and all other names with the same spiritual meaning.

Divine will is aptly named because the word divine is universal for "of God".

Gratitude opens this door as well.

Quantum/God - The second tool you are given at birth is Jesus. This one throws a lot of people off and its understandable considering the past track record of information concerning the man, the myth, and the Legend. Nonetheless, He is a tool, well more like tools. Jesus is the shield, the sword, the armor, the arrow, the healing and the Way.

I have to note here, I was a little shell shocked when I discovered the truth of Jesus. Meaning I found information, people and old books to educate myself on the teachings, the man, the myth and the Christ. I think most people will be moved to know the truth, at least that's my belief and my hope.

So here is the short, short version. A man was born, he was begotton [sexually reproduced by] Mary, wife of Joseph, and by God. This union created the man who was named Jesus before his birth by an Angel, read: messenger from God. This boy grew up in the time when God was not sought by many. God was not known as God or as Love. God was many gods with many names everywhere in the world. This took place [actual time] over 2500 years ago. This boy grew up in a world where up to that point was a world of Man. This place had wars, fights, tyranny, slavery, sexual conquest, beasts ruling the known world according to their beliefs. This place put the strong first, the weak last and the women in categories like animals. Meaning: There were slaves, breeders, trophies, prizes, whores, prostitutes, sirens, and more. For Woman survived alongside Man up to that point. When Jesus hit 13 his change of consciousness catapulted forward. The boy became the man who became the Son. From here the story changes several times depending on the religious filter you are using. And here is what all of them agree on; the man who claimed to be the Son of God died by crucifixion. He wasn't "crucified" he died by crucifixion which entails four nails, two planks of wood and a shit ton of man power to raise the cross up as a sign of what happens to people here. Now there is some agreement on the manner in which Jesus, Son of God prior to his death, on how his punishment was administered. Read this as 'endured acts of torture.' They placed a crown of thorns on his head and wrote 'King of the Jews'. Then a soldier, Roman from most accounts, took his spear and pierced this man, now hanging on some wood, in his side. This is an important detail which ironically was not lost in the translation. Thus its existence and testimonies written on the account, indicate this wound most likely terminated the life on the cross. Read: helped him die faster.

These we know as the five wounds of Christ, or the Stigmata. Which by the way was a great movie. How did Jesus get on the cross? Answer: He knew he was betrayed and willingly waited to be arrested. Jesus rode a mule into his trial, torture, judgment, and execution on purpose.

Remember when Harry had to walk into the forest to meet Lord Voldemort? Harry had to make the choice, no one else could. Harry was given everything he needed to survive that encounter. The knowledge, the experience, the philosopher's stone read: everlasting life. He dropped the stone and walked willingly to meet his death at the hand of the wizard who killed his parents.

Just as Neo stopped running when Agent Smith reappeared in the hallway and he stopped thier bullets with a word.

Jesus chose to die. He accepted his place and went for it with open arms. Now, the question I had was why? Who gave this guy the ability to do that and please, I pray tell me, why did he do it? He had it all. He had money, gifts, divine will, love, family, and the ability to rule all the known world. He gave it all up in the space of 30 years, a short life on this earth. Why? Why would any Man do that? For me that question is real, I mean serious. No man ever did more than he did for himself. He kept his lot, he chose the place and he enacted all rules, punishments and joys. No man would give up his own to give to another. I know because my step-father, grandfather, grandfather, uncles, cousins all took what they wanted, when they wanted it and gave us the scraps while belittling my existence. So why? Why would this man with all this power suddenly decide to end his life.?

I waited for my answer. I waited a long time. I haven't even asked it when I got the answer I sought. Because NO Man could ever tell me that and get an answer he was expecting. Not even close, bub. In fact, it would be better, for you, if you just stayed over there and didn't speak. For you have no power here, anymore. Nor do you deserve it for the wickedness in your hearts is what got Us here. Now, that I know Him, who He was, and what HE REALLY DID for me, for you, for everyone who has lived, will live and is living. I have to forgive YOU, for what you have done TO Me and Mine.

See, that sounds, like some bullshit man made up so he could keep raping, killing, enslaving, molesting, and selling women.

That is what I hear. I hear that because it was what I was TAUGHT, from birth. Not with just words, that can be dismissed by the wave of your nonchalant hand. No, taught as in beaten into, thrust upon, made to endure, and above all never speak of it. We call that, programming, my dears. Programming that created every problem, political issue, debate of the hour, and the combination of 2019,20,21 and 22. There is nothing here you haven't created, Man. Nothing. All of this, save the Earth, Sun, Moon, and the galaxy. We created. We made war on our neighbors. We made war on our People. We made WAR on our CHILDREN. We did. We also created all the laws and rules of society, not God. I am sure some of you believe the rules you have are inspired by God but the truth is nothing here is made by God. Save, You, the birds and the bees and the flowers and the trees.

When Jesus died on the cross that banned any further Sacrifice. Only now everyone knows they are the children of God and suddenly everyone wants to own everything. Enter War, Crusades, etc. The last tool is You.

Yes I gain a perverse laugh by calling people tools. Although its only funny because people created the word and then its different meanings. I am the asshole for using it correctly. C'est la Vie.

Tools need to be maintained, sharped, oiled, worked, and sometimes improved upon. Which can mean take some off or put some on.

The reason you are a Tool is because you are malleable, fluid, the existence of the most high God in corporeal form. If you knew this from the beginning then we would never have fought each other. Seeing as how that's not what happened then you, the tool, must know and experience this world to affect its perpetual existence.

The nature of the beast is to survive by any means possible. The beast is in you, your personal evolution spiritually. Once you know that the man created mythology was to scare you straight, well then you know it's always been you that controls your fate.

We change our perspective and we change the world.

BOOKS BY THIS AUTHOR

The Point Of Origin

The first in this series describing the consciousness of humanity. A grounding point to began the karmic journey of healing. The author's begining journey is included in this title.

www.ingramcontent.com/pod-product-compliance
Lightning Source LLC
LaVergne TN
LVHW050345160826
845677LV00014B/3792

* 9 7 9 8 8 3 2 5 6 0 8 4 7 *